4-8

D0475161

Hernan Cortes: Conquistador in Mexico

John Wilkes

Published in cooperation with Cambridge University Press
Lerner Publications Company, Minneapolis

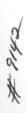

Editors' Note: In preparing this edition of *The Cambridge Topic Books* for publication, the editors have made only a few minor changes in the original material. In some isolated cases, British spelling and usage were altered in order to avoid possible confusion for our readers. Whenever necessary, information was added to clarify references to people, places, and events in British history. An index was also provided in each volume.

Spanish accents have been omitted in this book for the sake of simplicity, though Spaniards would write Cortés to show that the accent is on the second syllable. Aztec names are the nearest the English alphabet can get to the Aztec sounds. The familiar spelling of Montezuma has been used.

LIBRARY OF CONGRESS CATALOGING IN PUBLICATION DATA

Wilkes, John.
  Hernan Cortes: conquistador in Mexico.

  (A Cambridge Topic Book)
  Includes index.
  SUMMARY: A brief biography of the sixteenth-century Spanish conquistador, focusing on his role in the invasion and destruction of the Aztec civilization in Mexico.

  1. Cortés, Hernando, 1485-1547—Juvenile literature. 2. Mexico—Governors—Biography—Juvenile literature. 3. Explorers—Mexico—Biography—Juvenile literature. 4. Mexico—History—Conquest, 1519-1540—Juvenile literature. [1. Cortés, Hernando, 1485-1547. 2. Explorers] I. Title.

  F1230.C9397W54 1977   972'.02'0924 [B] [92]   76-22436
  ISBN 0-8225-1205-X

This edition first published 1977 by Lerner Publications Company
by permission of Cambridge University Press.

Original edition copyright © 1974 by Cambridge University Press
as part of *The Cambridge Introduction to the History of Mankind: Topic Book.*

International Standard Book Number: 0-8225-1205-X
Library of Congress Catalog Card Number: 76-22436

Manufactured in the United States of America.

This edition is available exclusively from:
Lerner Publications Company, 241 First Avenue North, Minneapolis, Minnesota 55401

Contents

Cortes, aged forty-five, and at the height of his power.

1 Cortes grows up in Spain

Hernan Cortes was born in Medellin, a small town in Extremadura, part of the kingdom of Castile. His father, Martin Cortes de Monroy, lived in retirement on his estates. Once he had been a captain of cavalry. The family was respectable and some distant relatives were famous, but it was far from rich.

We know very little about Hernan's childhood; indeed we cannot say whether his year of birth was 1484 or 1485. His mother, Catalina Altamirano, is supposed to have been religious and rather a hard woman, though this too is very uncertain. His parents certainly cared enough about him to send him off to the University of Salamanca when he was about fourteen years old. This was around the normal age of entry to

left: Salamanca University. This elaborate doorway was built in 1523.

below left: The wide, harsh landscape of Extremadura.

Spain at the end of the fifteenth century

KINGDOM OF FRANCE

KINGDOM OF CASTILE

KINGDOM OF ARAGON

● Salamanca

KINGDOM OF PORTUGAL

Medellin ●

Toledo ●

EXTREMADURA

R. Guadiana

R. Guadalquivir

● Seville

Granada ●

Sanlucar de Barrameda

Algiers

| 0 | 50 | 100 | 150 | Miles |
| 0 | 100 | 200 | 300 | Kilometres |

N

universities at that time. He lodged with his aunt and studied law.

Cortes left the university after two years without taking his degree. He had picked up some law and perhaps enough Latin to impress ignorant people but he was not really a university-educated man.

He was then faced with the need to earn a living. He was too proud to do manual work or become a trader because he was an *hidalgo* – a Spanish gentleman by birth – but as happened to many hidalgos, his family estates did not provide enough money to support him. If he had finished his university studies he might have served the king as a lawyer or a government official, but this was not possible.

The only career left to a gentleman was soldiering. His parents were distressed because they knew the respect that being a lawyer could bring. Cortes himself found it difficult to settle down to anything for long and soldiering suited him. He had been bred up to the life because Extremadura was a hard province. Generations of its menfolk had served the kings of Spain in the great wars against the Moors.

left: A narrow escape for the young Cortes. The man of the house would have run the 'burglar' through. But his mother-in-law persuades him to find out who the young man really is.

In 1492 the Moorish kingdom of Granada surrendered and the soldiers had to find something else to do. Soon, in 1494, great wars began in Italy but before that, in the very year 1492, Columbus had sighted the West Indies. The way was open for brave men to build a new Spanish empire overseas.

Cortes missed one chance to join. In 1502 Nicholas de Ovando, a family friend, was appointed governor of the island of Hispaniola, which was the centre of all Spanish activity in the New World. He offered Cortes a place on his staff. Cortes did not go because he was ill (he had fallen from a wall while trying to visit a girl friend secretly and was nearly killed by the enraged owner). When he was better he thought of volunteering for the Spanish army serving in Italy. He changed his mind –

we do not know why – and instead wandered round Spain. Eventually he took a job as a lawyer's clerk in Seville. Perhaps this reminded him of his old opportunity, for Seville was the place at which voyages of trade and exploration were planned and where they normally began.

He made up his mind at last. In 1504 he sailed for Hispaniola.

In the sixteenth century Seville was the great headquarters of trade with the New World. This picture was probably painted by Sancho Coello in the late fifteenth century.

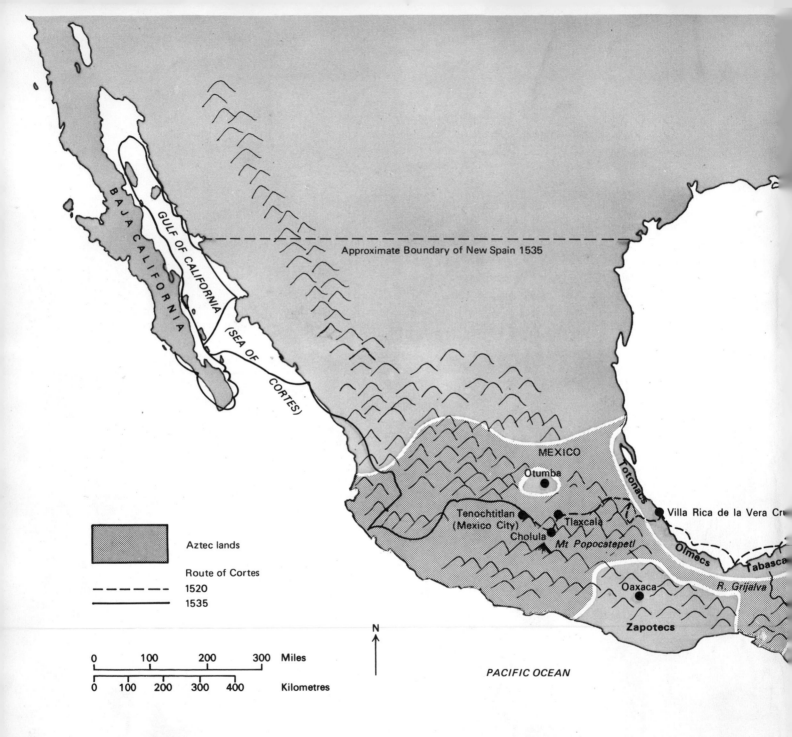

Approximate Boundary of New Spain 1535

GULF OF CALIFORNIA

BAJA CALIFORNIA

(SEA OF CORTES)

MEXICO

Otumba

Tenochtitlan
(Mexico City)

Tlaxcala

Cholula

Mt Popocatepetl

Totonacs

Villa Rica de la Vera Cru

Olmecs

Tabasca

R. Grijalva

Oaxaca

Zapotecs

Aztec lands

Route of Cortes

- - - - 1520

————— 1535

| 0 | 100 | 200 | 300 | Miles |

| 0 | 100 | 200 | 300 | 400 | Kilometres |

N

PACIFIC OCEAN

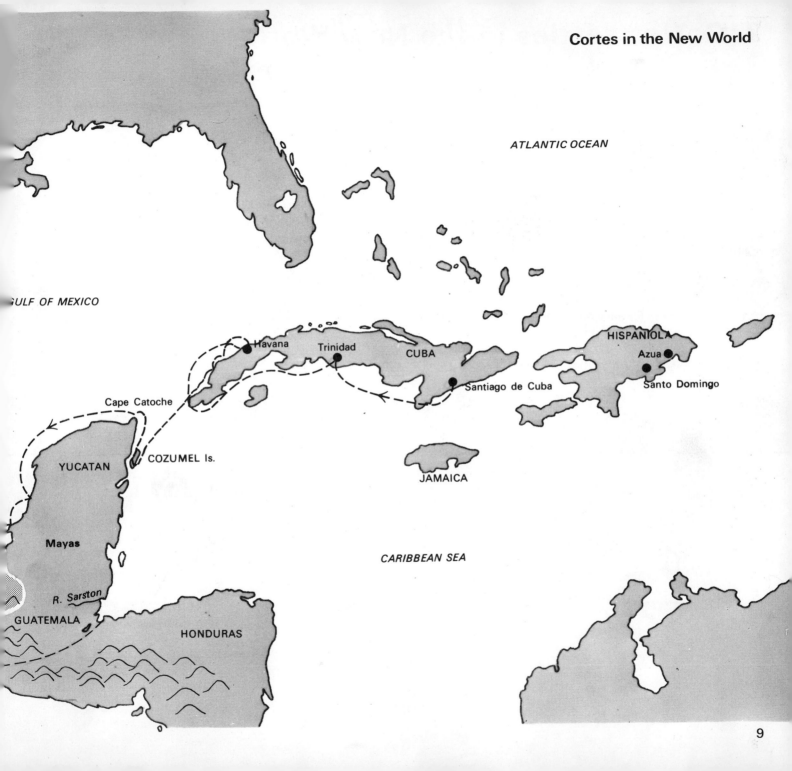

ATLANTIC OCEAN

GULF OF MEXICO

Havana

Trinidad

CUBA

HISPANIOLA

Azua

Santiago de Cuba

Santo Domingo

Cape Catoche

COZUMEL Is.

YUCATAN

JAMAICA

Mayas

CARIBBEAN SEA

R. Sarston

GUATEMALA

HONDURAS

2 Cortes settles in the New World

Nicholas de Ovando was still governor of Hispaniola when Cortes arrived on the island. He gave him a friendly welcome but little help at first.

Cortes began by gold mining. The rivers of Hispaniola carried gold, which was collected by the Taino people, who had inhabited Hispaniola before the Spanish conquest. The Spaniards treated them with such cruelty and overworked them so much that they were dying out. Partly through labour shortage, and partly because easily obtained deposits were becoming exhausted, less and less gold was being found. Cortes did not do better than anyone else and was soon so poor that he could not even afford a cloak of his own, and had to share one jointly with two friends.

He took a job as a lawyer in the small town of Azua, near the capital Santo Domingo. He worked mainly for the government, drawing up documents and contracts and seeing that Spanish law was kept thousands of miles from home. Ovando rewarded him with land and labourers to work for him. Slowly he began to make money, but he spent it on fine clothes and treating his friends. He was unmarried but not lonely.

Such a man did not settle easily under Ovando's firm rule. His restless nature wanted more adventure and when the chance came he was ready. Bernal Diaz, a soldier who served with Cortes, wrote a history of his adventures. He said this of Cortes, 'he was a ladies' man, and several times fought and always defeated brave and experienced men over this. He had a knife scar close to his lower lip though he covered it with his beard.'

Diego Velasquez, born between 1461 and 1466, was one of the earliest colonists in the New World, sailing on Columbus's second voyage. He was thus one of the most experienced and successful men in the Indies and a dangerous enemy to Cortes. He died in 1524.

The conquest of Cuba

In 1511 Ovando ordered an important settler in Hispaniola named Diego Velasquez to lead an expedition to conquer and settle the nearby island of Cuba. Velasquez looked around for energetic men to help him and chose Cortes as one of his officers. They were friends at this time, but later Velasquez became Cortes's worst enemy.

Cuba was conquered fairly easily. Cortes took his share of the land and profits of the island. He went into partnership with a trader and began to make money. It is said that he was the first man to see the opportunities of cattle ranching in Cuba, and imported the first beasts himself.

Cortes becomes a leader

Diego Velasquez was not content with Cuba. He wanted to conquer new lands in the king's name so that he would be rewarded with fame and a large share of the profits. He believed, like most Spaniards, that the Americas were stuffed with gold and it was only a matter of finding it. In 1517 and 1518 he fitted out expeditions to explore the peninsula of Yucatan. Both expeditions were discouraged by disease, and attacks from the people of Yucatan, though the survivors brought some gold and enough information to make a third expedition worth sending.

Velasquez had a problem. Whenever the Spaniards conquered a new country the largest prizes usually went to the leader of the conquerors. Velasquez could not leave Cuba. Therefore he had to choose someone who would stay loyal to him and come back to Cuba. Then Velasquez could write to the king claiming that he was the man who should really be rewarded since the leader of the expedition was just a hired soldier.

He had to find someone who seemed loyal but was intelligent and brave enough to lead a third expedition where the previous two had been failures.

He asked his secretary Andres de Duero and other trusted advisers. They suggested Cortes. It seemed good advice. Cortes was clearly brave, popular and efficient but not big enough to become a rival to the governor. It was a dreadful mistake. Velasquez did not know that for months Cortes had been working on de Duero and the others, bribing and persuading, so as to be made leader of the third expedition. On the surface all was casual and friendly, but underneath Cortes never stopped working for what he wanted.

Cortes changed his whole way of life as soon as Velasquez had appointed him. He began to dress in the rich clothes of an important leader – silks and velvets, with a gold chain around his neck. He rushed about collecting ships and recruiting men so quickly that the expedition was on the point of sailing before Velasquez realised that he had appointed a man who would never obey his orders again. He listened to Cortes's enemies. He became more and more suspicious but it was too late to stop the expedition. All he could do was to put as many men of his own in the army, telling them to stop Cortes from becoming independent if they possibly could.

Cortes realised that the next step would be his dismissal. He forestalled this by setting out at once, even though things were not quite ready. He sailed round the island of Cuba, calling at Trinidad and Havana to gather more men and more supplies. Velasquez sent word to have him arrested but the men of Havana took no notice. Velasquez had grown fat and careless as he aged and was forgetting that a leader has to earn loyalty and respect. Cortes also used his own power of personality on the doubters. He made them think he was the only man with enough skill and energy to make a success of the expedition. Did they want to be led by a second-rater? The expedition went on – and Diego roared out loud with rage like a bull when he heard that his orders had been disobeyed.

He was powerless. Cortes was out of his reach. He had sailed in mid-February, 1519, to the island of Cozumel, off the coast of Yucatan. He had 11 ships with 100 sailors. There were 508 soldiers, including 32 crossbowmen and 13 musketeers, 16 horses and about 14 small cannon.

Geronimo de Aguilar

One day Cortes heard some islanders of Cozumel using Spanish words. He realised they might have learned them from earlier explorers whom they had saved from shipwreck. Some of these explorers might even still be alive on the mainland. One such man actually joined them. His name was Geronimo de Aguilar and he had been shipwrecked in 1511 and enslaved, though later he had become one of the leaders of his tribe. Aguilar was a clergyman, intelligent and well-educated and glad to rejoin fellow Christians once more. At least one other Spaniard was heard of, but he refused to leave his Indian wife and adopted tribe.

Aguilar was most valuable to Cortes as an interpreter of the local language. From then on he was a full member of the expedition and accompanied the fleet as it sailed from Cozumel to the mouth of the Tabasco river. It was then March, 1519.

The departure. Cortes promises his men land, gold and power in Mexico: 'This war will be fought in God's name and faith. He will give us victory. More profit will come to our king and nation from our expedition than those of all the others. I will make you the richest of all men who have crossed the seas.'

A beach in Yucatan

3 On the coast of Mexico

Cortes did not get a peaceful reception. The landing place had been visited before, in 1518. The Tabascans had been friendly. Neighbouring tribes had accused them of being too cowardly to fight Spaniards. When Cortes appeared they decided to wipe out their neighbours' insults by fighting as hard as they could.

Battles went on for a few days, with the Spaniards losing four men killed, and the Tabascans many more. Eventually they were prepared to make peace.

As soon as things settled down Cortes behaved as he was always to do in Mexico. He was very friendly and gave presents. He talked to as many people as he could about Christianity and tried to persuade the natives to be baptised and set up altars. But he also took possession of the land in the name of the king of Spain.

This was done by reading a solemn document, planting a flag, or even marking a tree with sword cuts. His secretaries wrote down what happened.

As far as the Spaniards were concerned their king was the lawful ruler of all such lands, and the native peoples were as much subjects of the king of Spain as any Spaniard. It is very doubtful if the Indians understood either Christianity or the loss of their independence. Even the Spanish name for them, *Indios,* showed a misunderstanding. Columbus believed in 1492 that he had landed in Asia. He called the people he met Indians. By 1519 the Spaniards understood that they had not found Asia but a new continent altogether. Yet the old name stuck. The islands of the Caribbean became the West Indies and the inhabitants Indians. Cortes used the same name for the people he met in Yucatan and the rest of Mexico, even though they had nothing to do with the Indians of Asia or the Indians who were later discovered in the northern part of America.

The Indians could hardly have thought that the Spaniards would stay long in Mexico, let alone take the country over. So some tribes welcomed them because of their own problems. Their basic complaint was that they were not free.

Cortes learned that in the interior of Mexico lived a people called the Aztecs. The Aztec emperor (as the Spaniards called him) was named Montezuma. The Aztecs had conquered vast areas of Mexico but had then left the defeated peoples alone, as long as they paid tribute. The Aztecs took corn, chili, cacao, to eat; copper bracelets and gold ornaments to wear; jade and turquoise to clothe the statues of their gods; quetzal feathers for the emperor. These demands were sometimes heavy, but far worse was the Aztec thirst for human lives. They slaughtered hundreds every year as human sacrifices to their gods.

Cortes saw his chance. He promised to free the other Indians from Aztec rule, provided they swore loyalty instead to his emperor, Charles V. The Indians did so, hardly understanding that this oath meant they had really exchanged one hard master for another. In addition, Cortes saw that, having once supported him and fought against the Aztecs, they could not desert him. For if the Spaniards were defeated and killed, the revenge of Montezuma would destroy their towns and villages and drag them to the altars for sacrifice.

Marina

When peace had been made the Tabascans gave Cortes some women as slaves. To his surprise Cortes found that one of these was from another part of Mexico and could speak Nahuatl, the language of the Aztecs themselves. This was a tremendous stroke of luck.

The Spaniards called this woman Marina (or Malinche) probably a corruption of her Aztec name *Malinal*. She was an intelligent woman. She translated from Nahuatl into a local language which Aguilar could understand and translate into Spanish. Later she learned Spanish herself. She was absolutely loyal to Cortes (indeed she became his mistress and had his child) and could explain how the Indians were thinking as well as what they said.

Marina and Aguilar translate, as Cortes receives a present from a chief.

Cortes receives the
Aztec ambassadors.

16

First meeting with the Aztecs

Far away in the Aztec capital, the great city of Tenochtitlan, news of the strangers had reached Montezuma. Orders went out to investigate and report. On the weekend of Easter, 1519 the Aztec provincial governor and other ambassadors arrived on the coast.

Everything appeared calm and peaceful, although the coastal Indians never ceased to warn Cortes about the treacherous Aztecs. Cortes received feathered cloaks and other beautiful things. The Spaniards offered shirts, beads and an armchair for Montezuma. Then the Spaniards put on a display of firepower, which amazed the Indians. Cortes also held a service on the beach and lectured the Indians on the Catholic faith.

At the same time each side was getting on with its real aims. Cortes tried to persuade the ambassadors to allow him to travel to Tenochtitlan and meet Montezuma. The ambassadors refused and said they wanted the Spaniards to leave Mexico.

Aztec artists drew careful pictures of Cortes and all his men, the horses (which fascinated them) and everything to do with the Spaniards, even down to their greyhounds. The ambassadors also gave their own accounts. We know from later Aztec historians how puzzled they were to account for things so strange: 'Their deer carry them on their backs wherever they wish to go. These deer are as tall as the roof of a house ... As for their food it is like human food.' They spoke also of 'A thing like a ball of fire comes out of its stomach; it comes out shooting sparks and raining fire ... it shatters a tree into splinters, a most unnatural sight, as if the tree had exploded from within.'

About thirty years after Cortes landed, Bernadino de Sahagun wrote about what happened. Pictures of the events were drawn by an Indian artist. This one shows Cortes and his men landing on the beach and meeting the Aztecs. The Indian artist shows several scenes in one picture and takes care to make some details very clear. Compare this with a modern artist's picture shown on the opposite page.

Cortes makes a great decision

Shortly after the ambassadors left Cortes made the greatest decision of his life. Even though the ambassadors had made it clear that he would not be welcome he decided to march to Tenochtitlan and meet the Aztec emperor, Montezuma. Cortes had thus made up his mind to plunge an unknown distance into an unknown country where hundreds of thousands of warriors dwelt. He did not know how he would be received or whether he could return. He could take only 400 men. There would be no chance of outside help if he was trapped by the Aztecs.

Nevertheless this was his plan. Why did he decide to take such risks? You may think of many reasons; here are a few. We know Cortes was tremendously ambitious, even to risking his life for fame. We know also he was genuinely religious. Perhaps he thought that as the Spaniards were doing God's work in converting the Indians then God would protect them. The Spaniards were revolted by human sacrifice and could hardly believe God would stop them from ending it.

There were also less honourable reasons. The Aztecs had already shown by their presents that they lived in a rich country. To be able to take over such a country was a gambler's dream – and Cortes was always prepared to gamble. Above all was the gold. Cortes himself is supposed to have said something that

sums up what the conquistadors were really like. 'I and my companions suffer from a disease of the heart which can only be cured with gold.'

These may have been the reasons and the dreams which took him into the interior of Mexico.

The break with Velasquez

When Cortes's men realised what he intended to do not all of them were in favour. Some said that Cortes would 'send them to the slaughterhouse'. Others took courage and followed him, but Diego Velasquez's men were furious. They knew that Cortes planned to disobey his orders (which were to stay on the coast, trade with the natives and then return to Cuba). They tried to persuade the soldiers to force Cortes to abandon his plan.

Cortes outwitted them. He kept very calm and talked to the soldiers, pointing out that if they went back to Cuba they would have no land in Mexico and little gold, for Velasquez would claim it for the king of Spain and for himself. He asked them

There were many civilisations in what is now Mexico during the centuries before Cortes arrived. This pyramid at El Tajin on the coast north of Cempoala had been standing for at least 1000 years. It is now known as the pyramid of the 364 niches. Each niche may have contained a carved statue.

what use their sufferings would have been if they returned empty-handed. They began to think again.

Next Cortes set about founding a town near the Spanish camp. It was only a plan worked out on the ground and a few shacks, but he gave it the splendid name of Villa Rica de la Vera Cruz – the Rich Town of the True Cross.

This may sound absurd but was really very clever. For centuries when any Spaniards conquered a new region they always set up towns, with proper town councillors, policemen and officials. Then the king approved what they had done and usually rewarded them. Town councillors were the king's servants and to disobey them was rebellion. The councillors of

Vera Cruz (who were all Cortes's friends) then appointed him general of the army and governor of what they called New Spain, that is, the land of Mexico. If Velasquez's men disobeyed Cortes he could write to the king and say they were rebels. He could also say that Velasquez had told him only to trade, but he had given the king a whole new country, rich in gold, land and men. Charles V could hardly turn down such a gift.

Cortes wrote a long letter to the Emperor Charles V, explaining what he had done. The letter still survives, in Vienna. It is cunningly written. Cortes did not lie, but he left out part of the truth. Charles V had appointed Velasquez to be governor of Cuba and Cortes had no right to disobey Velasquez.

Cortes was gambling. He hoped that if his expedition was successful and he sent back gold to Charles V, the emperor would forgive him for disobeying Velasquez. This was dangerous, because Velasquez had powerful friends at court in Spain. As soon as Cortes's letter reached Charles V they told him the letter was a lie and Cortes a rebel. Cortes's father Martin came to defend his son. Everything depended on Charles's decision. Charles's decision itself depended on news from Mexico. But letters took weeks to travel across the Atlantic ocean.

Velasquez heard about Cortes's letter from a spy who deserted the ship he sent to Spain. He was beside himself with rage and immediately set about collecting an army to pursue Cortes to Mexico and stop his disobedience. He made his friend Panfilo de Narvaez commander. But long before Narvaez reached Vera Cruz, Cortes had marched into Mexico.

Before he marched, he made sure that nobody would desert. He 'discovered' that his remaining ships were worm-eaten, and had them all run aground. (The expression 'burning your boats' comes from this incident.) There could be no retreat.

The photograph above shows part of a letter which Cortes wrote to Charles V. It tells of Montezuma's welcoming speech. The letters of Cortes were soon printed, because many people in Europe loved to read about exploration in the New World. The picture on the right shows the title page of the first edition of Cortes' second letter. It was printed in Seville in 1522 and has a drawing of the emperor.

4 Cortes gains allies: the march to Tenochtitlan

Cortes had learned much during his four months on the coast of Mexico. He chose a route to Tenochtitlan which took him through the lands of tribes who hated the Aztecs, so as to bring them on to his own side. The journey was long and hard. Mexico is a very mountainous country and the Spaniards were racked with disease. Eventually they reached the country of the Tlaxcalans.

The people were fierce warriors. They had never been conquered by the Aztecs, who preferred to attack them from time to time to capture warriors for sacrifice. Although the Tlaxcalans hated the Aztecs, they were equally suspicious of the Spaniards. Their war chief Xicotenga was for fighting and the Spaniards had to endure a series of sharp battles. Eventually the council of chiefs was convinced that Cortes was really an enemy of Montezuma and decided to join him.

This was vital to the Spaniards. Tlaxcalans proved the most loyal and successful of Cortes's allies. They, and thousands of Indians from other peoples, formed a vast auxiliary army, fighting with the Spaniards, offering their towns as fortresses and headquarters, providing porters and labourers to carry everything the army needed. It is very unlikely that the Spaniards would have succeeded if the peoples of Mexico had been united against them. History books often mention that only four or five hundred Spaniards went on the first march to Tenochtitlan. They should also add that at least 20,000 Indians were there fighting on the Spanish side.

Day by day the combined army drew nearer Tenochtitlan. They climbed into the highlands of Mexico, the 'cold land' which killed Indians from the coast and brought chills and fever to everyone. Even there a spirit of brave enquiry did not desert them. Some found the strength to climb the towering volcano, Popocateptl. This greatly impressed the Indians, who thought that demons lived in the 'smoking mountain'.

Sick with dysentery and fearful of what lay ahead, the

above right: Popocatepetl, 17,887 feet (5453 m) high, the great 'Smoking Mountain' of the Aztecs, on the road to Tenochtitlan. The volcano's crater is 5165 ft (1574 m) in diameter and nearly 1000 ft (304.8 m) deep.

This tropical scene near Oaxaca shows the type of rough country Cortes encountered as he journeyed inland. The maguey cactus (foreground) provided paper, needles and thread for the Aztecs.

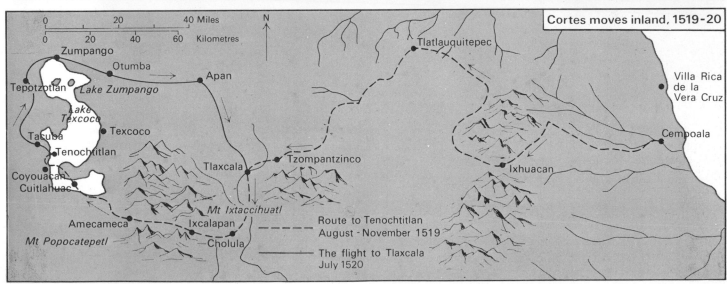

Cortes moves inland, 1519-20

Zumpango

Otumba

Apan

Tepotzotlan

Lake Zumpango

Lake Texcoco

Texcoco

Tacuba

Tenochtitlan

Coyouacan

Cuitlahuac

Amecameca

Mt Ixtaccihuatl

Ixcalapan

Cholula

Mt Popocatepetl

Tlaxcala

Tzompantzinco

Tlatlauquitepec

Villa Rica de la Vera Cruz

Cempoala

Ixhuacan

N

0   20   40 Miles

0   20   40   60 Kilometres

Route to Tenochtitlan
August - November 1519

The flight to Tlaxcala
July 1520

A wooden spear-thrower nearly 5 ft (1.5 m) long, with decorated finger-grips made of shell.

left: The Aztecs often made masks of the faces of their gods. This is Tlaloc, god of rain. The mask is a mosaic of mother-of-pearl and semi-precious stones. Tlaloc's tongue sticks out to lap up rain water. Sometimes masks were built on real human skulls.

opposite: A 'bird's-eye view' of Tenochtitlan. The roads leading into the city, the network of canals and buildings, can easily be seen. The great temples dominate the city. Cortes and his men entered by the southern causeway (on the right of this picture).

Spaniards struggled over the last mountain pass and gazed down on the valley of Mexico and one of the wonders of the world – Tenochtitlan, the capital city of the Aztecs.

The entry into Tenochtitlan

The city was built on islands in the shallow lake which then spread over much of the valley of Mexico. It was joined to the mainland by several causeways, each about 23 feet (7 metres) wide. The Spaniards marched from their camp along the cause-way through vast crowds of Aztecs who had turned out to see them and many more travellers to and from the city. Hundreds of canoes floated on the lake beside the causeway.

Bernal Diaz remembered that though the Spaniards were frightened they were also very proud. '... before us was the great city of Mexico. We were scarcely four hundred strong and we remembered the warnings of the people of Tlaxcala, to beware of entering the city, since the Mexicans would kill us as soon as they had us inside. What men in all the world have shown such daring?'

As the Spaniards drew nearer the city so their amazement grew. 'These great towns ... seemed like an enchanted vision. Some of our soldiers asked whether it was not all a dream.' 'It was all so wonderful that I do not know how to describe this first glimpse of things never heard of, seen or dreamed of before.'

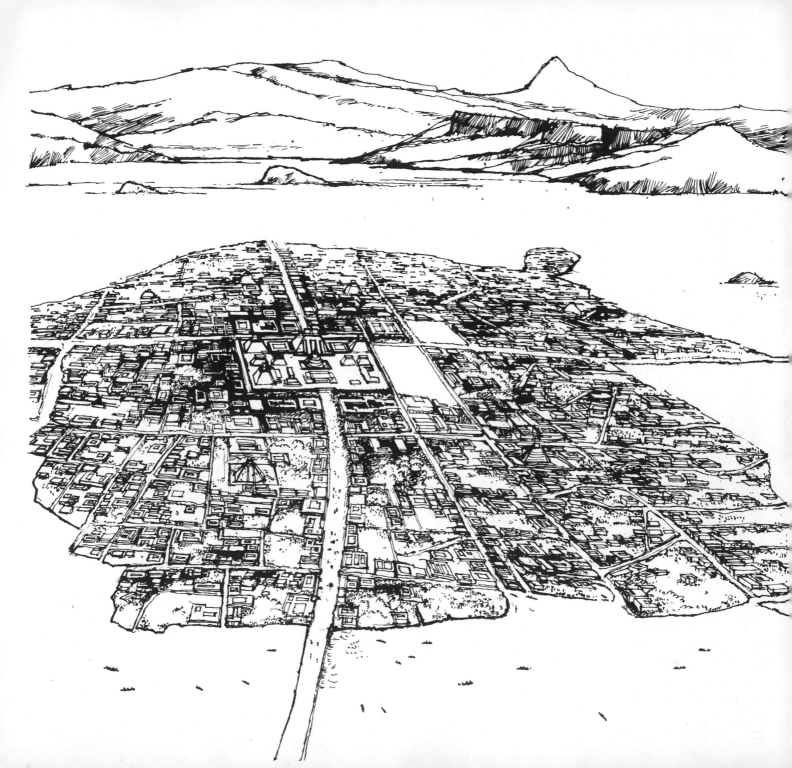

At the junction of two causeways, about half a mile from the city proper, the main Aztec reception began. Men of higher and higher rank appeared and then, at last, Montezuma himself. Lords carried a canopy over his head while others swept the road before him. All except the greatest kept their eyes bowed, never looking him in the face. Cortes saw who was coming and dismounted. Montezuma was helped out of his litter. The two men met. Cortes bowed and gazed for the first time at the man whose empire he would soon take away for ever.

The Spaniards were then given the palace of Montezuma's late father Axayacatl, close to the Emperor's own palace and the great temple, whose towers dominated the city.

For several days afterwards Cortes and Montezuma met, while the Spanish soldiers wandered about, totally amazed at the beauty, order and civilisation of Tenochtitlan. Canals separated the whitewashed houses; flowers and trees grew everywhere; great aqueducts brought fresh water to clean the spotless city. In his second long letter to the Emperor Charles V, Cortes himself takes pages to describe the skill of Montezuma's painters, jewellers and artisans. He wonders at the great market of the city, where 60,000 people bought food everyday. Only the unending stream of human sacrifices seems to horrify him.

Cortes captures Montezuma

On the face of things Cortes and Montezuma were friendly; underneath Cortes was making private plans. It was clear that Montezuma liked the Spaniards and perhaps feared them in a superstitious way, but was hardly likely to give up his empire freely. Some Aztec chiefs favoured killing the newcomers there and then. The stalemate could not last long.

Once Cortes made up his mind he acted without further hesitation, whatever the risk. He collected a few of his officers, went to the emperor's palace, and calmly told the astonished Montezuma that he was to go with the Spaniards to their palace, as a prisoner.

For hours the Spaniards tried to persuade Montezuma to hand himself over to them. Cortes used kind words but others were much blunter. Bernal Diaz remembered the high squeaky voice of one captain, 'What is the use of all these words? Either we take him or we knife him. If we do not look after ourselves we shall be dead men.' Eventually Montezuma gave in and walked with the Spaniards to their palace. He forbade his guards to touch them. From then on he conducted the government of his own country under Spanish guard. He protested only when Cortes tried to stop the human sacrifice in the great temple. A few days later, according to Spanish accounts of the affair, Montezuma actually surrendered his country to Cortes, as the representative of the Emperor Charles V. Everyone was moved to tears by the sadness of the occasion, the Spaniards reported solemnly. Hernan Cortes, at thirty-four years of age, had taken over an empire of millions.

Why did the Aztec emperor give way?

If only we knew the answer to this question! It is difficult to say what really happened. Cortes in his letters only wrote what suited him. He said Montezuma had handed over his empire quite freely because he believed Cortes had come from the Aztec gods.

It is true that the Aztecs had a prophecy that one of their gods would return and claim the land and people of Mexico again. It is also true that Montezuma was a very religious man. But he had spent some time very close to the Spaniards. Could he still have believed they were divine? Other Aztecs don't seem to have imagined any such thing. Perhaps the Spaniards threatened Montezuma? Yet he needed to say only one word and his guards would have killed Cortes on the spot. He was not just a coward. Bernal Diaz, who helped to guard him, agrees with other writers that he was always a brave, dignified man, who never forgot he was the emperor of a fighting people.

The most likely explanation is that Montezuma simply miscalculated. He probably believed that he was safe in his own city and that he could have the Spaniards killed at any time he chose. Secondly, the Spaniards were ambassadors from Charles V and the Aztecs were civilised people who did not kill ambassadors. Finally, the gloomy Aztec religion had a powerful influence over Montezuma. The Spaniards had come at a time when the priests expected disasters. Perhaps at the very back of his mind Montezuma was what is called a fatalist — that is, some one who believes that what is to come, will come. Therefore it was best to leave things to the gods. If the great war god Huitzilopochtli gave a sign, Montezuma would know, but until that sign came it was best to do nothing. We shall never know the truth because we do not have all the evidence, and the Aztec way of thinking is very difficult for us to understand.

5 The loss of Tenochtitlan

Cortes leaves the city

With Montezuma under house-arrest the Aztec lords began to realise that the Spaniards thought of themselves as the new rulers of Mexico. They also saw what kind of men had arrived amongst them. Years afterwards one of the Aztecs told what had begun to happen; we can still feel his disgust and hatred after four and a half centuries: 'They searched the treasure house, questioning and quarrelling, and seized every object they thought was beautiful. They went to Montezuma's storehouse where his personal treasures were kept. They grinned like little beasts and patted each other with delight. They seized these treasures as if they were their own. When they had taken all the gold, they heaped up everything else in the middle of the courtyard.'

At this moment, when the Aztecs were recovering from shock and tempers were rising, Cortes heard that Diego Velasquez was about to take his revenge. Panfilo de Narvaez, with 900 men and 20 cannon, had landed at Vera Cruz and was marching towards Tenochtitlan.

Cortes had to choose which danger to face. He decided to tackle Narvaez himself and leave Pedro de Alvarado, who was brave, popular, a proved leader of fighting men, and one of Cortes's strongest supporters, in charge of Mexico City. He set out for the coast.

Narvaez heard Cortes was on the way. He established a

'They grinned like little beasts . . . .'

Pedro de Alvarado (?1485–1541). A senior officer under Cortes, he was a veteran of two earlier expeditions to Yucatan. After the conquest of Mexico he fought mainly in Guatemala and what is now El Salvador. He founded the capital of Guatemala where he now lies buried. The portrait, probably painted later in the sixteenth century, shows him at the height of his power as governor of Guatemala.

Don
PEDRO DE
ALVARADO
Capitán Conquista-
dor de México. Co-
mendador en la Or-
den de Santiago Go-
bernador, Capitán
General, Adelantado
de Guatemala y su
fundador.
nació en Badajoz
murió en Jalisco.

fortified camp in an Indian temple. It was pouring with rain. Cortes as usual took advantage of the conditions. He overran the camp before Narvaez could rally his men. Narvaez lost one eye, put out by a pike, and was forced to surrender.

Cortes had sent messengers with bribes to some of Narvaez's men even before the battle had started. This was one reason why he overcame his rival without too much fighting. He then turned on all his powers of persuasion to recruit men to return with him to Tenochtitlan and continue the struggle against the Aztecs. Hundreds of fresh men agreed, especially when Cortes pointed out that they could hope for nothing from Velasquez if they went back to Cuba. Even Narvaez came with them, half blinded and broken in spirit by Cortes's cunning and power of personality. He was not in Cortes's class as a leader and years later was still sad and confused when he tried to work out why he had lost.

Cortes also took precautions against his enemies in Spain. He wrote to the king saying that Velasquez and Narvaez had defied the king's officials in Cuba by launching an expedition to punish Cortes. He also claimed that Narvaez had taken no notice of the council of Vera Cruz, which would make him twice a rebel. What Cortes did *not* say, of course, was that the council of Vera Cruz had not been approved by the king, and that Cortes was defying Velasquez's orders in the first place!

Although Cortes had defeated Narvaez in Mexico he could not even take part in the real battle, which was going on around the Emperor Charles V. This was a battle where the weapons were letters – from Velasquez, from other royal officials in the New World, and from Cortes himself. Lies and bribes were used by Cortes's friends and enemies alike at court to persuade the emperor as to who was really working for him in Mexico, and who was a rebel, defying his king and taking away profits which Charles should have been collecting. Cortes knew that even if he won every battle in Mexico the day could come when he would lose all he had gained, if the emperor ever decided

left: An Aztec drum. It is decorated with signs of the calendar, representing time, and eagles, symbols of war. Captives were sacrificed to the sound of drums like these. This one is 2 ft 11 in (88 cm) high.

that Velasquez was right and Cortes wrong. This is why even when things were at their worst in Mexico he never lost sight of the need to keep Charles informed. He was looking ahead – towards the day after his victory.

Alvarado makes the Aztecs rebel

If Narvaez's army had known what had happened in Tenochtitlan while Cortes was away they would not have been so keen to join him. Pedro de Alvarado was strong, and daring – the Indians nicknamed him 'the Sun', a great compliment. He was loyal to Cortes, but he lacked Cortes's political skill and sense of timing. Cortes knew when to strike and when to be patient. Since the Spaniards were surrounded by Aztecs, and did not know if Cortes was alive or dead, it was clearly a time to wait and see what help they could hope to receive. But Alvarado became certain that the Aztecs were planning to rise and kill him and his men before Cortes returned. He said Marina had warned him that the rising would come during the ceremony called the 'Feast of Flowers' when Aztec nobles came to dance and sing in the palace courtyard. He therefore decided to strike first and kill these men.

Alvarado's story may be true. The Aztecs seem to have had a great respect for Cortes and perhaps they thought that it would be easier to get rid of the Spaniards while he was out of the city. Maybe the Tlaxcalans saw a wonderful opportunity to have their old enemies killed by the Spaniards – so they persuaded Marina that there was an Aztec plot.

Whatever the real story we do know that the dancers assembled in the courtyard and began the ceremony. Alvarado blocked every exit with soldiers and, terrible in their armour, he and his companions cut down the defenceless nobles.

The Aztecs rose immediately in rebellion. Men came fighting mad from all over the city. Alvarado managed to get his men back to the Spanish headquarters after a savage fight, using cannon at short range to blow crowds to bits.

Aztec artists drew the massacre for a history of Mexico written by Frey Diego Duran in the sixteenth century but not published for 300 years. They also described the savagery of the Spaniards: 'They struck the arms of a man who beat the drums; they severed both his hands . . . of some they slashed open the back, the shoulder, and cut their bodies to pieces.'

Cortes was allowed back into the city, possibly because the Aztecs wanted all the Spaniards trapped in the same place, or because many of their leaders had been killed and they could not organise themselves quickly enough. Once he was in, the Aztecs surrounded and attacked the Spaniards in the palace more furiously than ever.

Then the end came for poor Montezuma. The Spaniards took him up to the roof of the palace to order the besieging Aztecs to stop fighting. The Aztecs were hurling stones at the roof and one of them hit him. His people may not have seen who it was, or perhaps some thought that he was a traitor. Cortes says he died from the effects of the blow, but there is another story that Cortes had him and other Aztec chiefs murdered. Montezuma's brother Cuitlahuac was elected war chief and the Aztec siege continued.

The 'noche triste'

The Spaniards soon realised that they were faced with the grim choice between starving to death and attempting to break out of the city against the force of the Aztec army. There could only be one answer; preparations began quickly. The share of

Montezuma's treasure which had been set aside for the Emperor Charles V was loaded on to a mare. Cortes told the troops and porters that anyone could take what he could carry from the rest of the treasure. Many men loaded themselves down with plunder, making it difficult even to stagger along. The Spaniards set out on a night in late June, (probably the 30th). They had built a portable bridge to help cross gaps in the causeway. Gonzalo de Sandoval led the long winding column and Alvarado commanded the rearguard. Cortes and a hundred cavalry rode up and down the line, ready to help where danger was greatest.

At first all was quiet and the Spaniards were hidden briefly by darkness and mist, but by the time they had begun to move along the causeway, towards the shore of the lake, day was breaking and they had been seen. The Aztecs were roused and waiting. Warriors poured on to the road behind the Spaniards while others shot at them from canoes. There were no men obstructing them, probably because they presented a fine target while exposed along the causeway, and they were steadily driven away from the Aztec capital.

Aztec cries for vengeance mingled with the war cry of

Castile, 'Santiago! Santiago!', and anguished prayers to God and the Saints. Whenever a Spaniard or a Tlaxcalan fell into the lake the Aztecs tried to drag him off, half-drowned, for sacrifice. Many others were cut down by Aztec battle maces.

No one knows how many died on that night. There were at least 600 Spaniards lost. The Indian dead, among Tlaxcalans on the Spanish side and among the Aztecs themselves, must have been very great. We cannot give an accurate estimate. Many of the Spaniards who died had come fresh to Tenochtitlan after being with Narvaez's army. They burdened themselves with so much gold that they could not defend themselves, and some even drowned in the lake rather than let go of their loot. 'They died rich,' said the old veterans sarcastically, 'and their gold killed them.' One of Montezuma's daughters died; two others survived and afterwards married Spaniards.

The battle of Otumba

The night of sorrows – *noche triste* to the Spaniards – was an experience which the survivors never forgot. It was as close as Cortes ever came to total defeat in Mexico. The following day as he sat by a great tree, weeping and praying, he must have felt that the worst was over. Probably nothing ever matched the terror of the night of sorrows, but the Aztecs did not cease to hunt his men by day and night. Starving, with wounded men clinging for support to the tails of the horses, the Spaniards struggled, like men drowning, to reach the safety of the border with Tlaxcala.

Meanwhile Montezuma's young nephew Cuauhtemoc was chosen emperor of the Aztecs. He was brave and determined, with none of Montezuma's worries about who the Spaniards really were and how they should be treated. About a week after the night of sorrows the largest Aztec army ever seen barred the Spaniards' way to Tlaxcala. The Aztec stand was made in the wide valley of Otumba and this gave some room for manoeuvre to the Spanish cavalry. For hours Cortes and his men cut and thrust at the packed Aztec ranks, striving all the time to keep moving and avoid being surrounded. The Indians fought equally fiercely, hacking and crushing with their maces and trying to grab Spaniards for sacrifice. Although the Spaniards had some guns and crossbows they had to rely mainly on the steel points of swords and lances, while their Tlaxcalan allies battled beside them with spear and club.

The Aztecs had overwhelming numbers, but also the serious problem of having to fight a completely new sort of battle. They had seen horses ever since the Spaniards came (at first some had thought horses as intelligent as men, others that horse and rider were one monstrous animal) and knew they could be killed. What they had never before faced was a full-scale charge by armoured cavalry. It needed a quite special kind of bravery to stand up to such weight and speed. Yet the Jaguar Knights and the Eagle Knights did just that, sometimes even trying to snatch at the lances and pitch riders off their horses.

Firearms were also quite new, and must have been very frightening.

As the battle went on the Aztecs found yet another danger. Their obsidian-edged maces were deadly sharp but also very brittle. After a time the blades became blunted against Spanish steel plate armour. The Aztecs (and some Spaniards) wore Indian armour of quilted cotton soaked in brine. This was much cooler than plate armour and could resist a battle mace, but it was useless against the steel *points* of Spanish weapons, which went straight through the thick cotton.

Finally the Aztecs were used to depending on their chiefs for leadership in battle. Many of these men must have been killed or wounded in earlier fighting, some others murdered by Alvarado, and it may be that the Aztec army was less efficient than usual.

In any event it was the Aztec reliance on leaders which did much to save the Spaniards and their friends. Bernal Diaz and others agree that Cortes himself charged down the Aztec

31

general, whose feathers and plumes made him a distinct target. This man's death so confused and discouraged the others that they broke off the battle.

A few days after the battle the Spanish army reached the safety of Tlaxcalan lands. They had been worried in case their defeat in Tenochtitlan had caused even the Tlaxcalans to

desert. This did not happen and so the army could regroup and the wounded survivors recover.

Cortes himself records that he had head wounds and had lost two fingers of his left hand. Many others were crippled and diseased. Bernal Diaz says that about 1,300 men had set out with Cortes to relieve Pedro de Alvarado, but that 860 of these

had been killed in all the battles since, or sacrificed, with another 70 men lost in a separate battle fought by some of Narvaez's men. It says a great deal for the endurance of the kind of men who fought in Mexico that they could stand up to warfare, disease, the hard marches and poor food of everyday living and yet fight back after such suffering.

The Battle of Otumba. Cortes and his cavalry fighting Eagle and Jaguar Knights. The Spaniards and their allies are beginning to break through the Aztec army towards safety.

6 Cortes fights back

It took nine months to prepare for the return to Tenochtitlan. Cortes did not need much time to work out a plan for a new campaign against the Aztecs, but many preparations had to be made.

First he ordered twelve small sailing boats to be built. The name for that kind of boat was 'brigantine'. Nails and rigging were brought from Vera Cruz and skilful Indian carpenters copied plans and boats they were shown.

Next Cortes spent months winning over cities and towns around the lake of Mexico and on the road between the lake and Vera Cruz. He did this so as to make sure that he would

The use of brigantines enabled the Spaniards to command the lake, and seal off Tenochtitlan.

not be attacked from the rear when he returned to Tenochtitlan itself, and also to cut off the places which might help the Aztecs when the war began. But why should the Indians join him? Firstly, Cortes was the only man able to offer them protection against the Aztecs, who had taken tribute and sacrifices for so long. He was very careful *always* to give this protection, so that any Indian city knew that if it rebelled against the Aztecs, there would be Spanish help. Secondly, many Indians were realising that the Spaniards were likely to turn on any city that did not help them, or that betrayed them. Punishment and protection were equally certain when they came from Cortes.

The brigantines were finished in the spring of 1521. Indian porters then dragged and carried them for the first miles overland. Then a canal was dug to link with the lake in the valley of Mexico. The boats were launched on the lake, and at the same time Cortes mustered his men. He wrote to Charles V that he had 700 infantry, 118 men with musket or crossbow, 86 cavalry and 15 cannon. Then he summoned the Tlaxcalans, who produced 25,000 men, obviously a vital part of the army.

Cortes divided his forces, so that Tenochtitlan could be attacked from several points at once. Two commanders, Gonzalo de Sandoval and Cristobal de Olid, first cut the aqueducts that supplied the city. A few days later, Spanish and Indian forces blocked each of the four causeways which linked Tenochtitlan with the mainland. The brigantines began to patrol the lake. The Aztecs were thus completely cut off.

Then the Spaniards and their Indian allies began a series of attacks along the causeways. They were trying to reach the city along these roads. Each day they moved forward, fighting the Aztecs as they went. Spanish engineers blocked up gaps in the causeways so that the army could bring up supplies. But there were times, especially at night, when the Spaniards drew back and the Aztecs regained stretches of causeway and opened up great gaps, which the Spaniards were forced to bridge next time they advanced. The brigantines also supported the army by fighting Aztec war canoes on the lake and helping the soliders fighting along the causeways. Each brigantine had musketeers and a small cannon which shot at the Aztecs in canoes and on the causeways.

At first the invaders made little progress. The Aztecs fought with unceasing courage, led by their elite warriors, the Eagle Knights and the Jaguar Knights. They used the cover of houses and temples very well. They were hard to pin down and the Spaniards were ambushed again and again.

One particular terror for the Spaniards was of being captured. The Aztecs never ceased to make human sacrifices even at the height of battle, and a Spaniard was especially prized.

Sometimes Spaniards fighting could even see their comrades dragged up the steps of the great temple, sacrificed, and their bodies hurled down to the square. All the time, as Bernal Diaz says, they were deafened and depressed by the non-stop booming of sacrificial drums echoing over the city, and the cries of victims.

Cortes then decided that the only way to win was to destroy the city, bit by bit, as each part was conquered. Every time a house or a temple was captured it was burned or knocked down, so that there was nowhere for the Aztecs to hide, or re-occupy if the Spaniards pulled back to camp for the night. Even the aviaries where Montezuma had kept hundreds of animals and birds were ruined. Cortes wrote to Charles V: 'Although it

The Aztec emperor tries to escape.

distressed me I made up my mind to burn them, for it distressed the enemy very much more; and they showed great grief.'

Cortes's plan was harsh but it worked. Each day the Aztecs lost ground and were jammed into a smaller space. They ran out of food and even ate the bark from the trees. Smallpox (caught from the Spaniards and deadly to Aztecs) now raged among them. At the end there was nowhere to tread or lie down except on the corpses of the unburied dead.

Starved, sick and desperate the men of Tenochtitlan refused to surrender until, early in August 1521, they could do no more.

They were finally trapped in the area around the great market place of Tlatelolco. Resistance ceased. The leader at this time was the eighteen-year-old Cuauhtemoc, who had fought to the last. He tried to escape by canoe with a band of warriors in order to lead resistance elsewhere, but he was seen, chased by one of the brigantines and recaptured. Tlaxcalans rampaged through the broken ruins of Tenochtitlan, slaughtering and enslaving the survivors. No one knows how many thousands had died over the seventy-five days of the seige. Of Spaniards over a hundred men had been killed, or captured or sacrificed by the Aztecs.

7 Hernan Cortes – lord of Mexico

Cortes first tackled the job of getting Mexico going again. The dead were buried and plans made for rebuilding Tenochtitlan, now renamed *Ciudad Mexico* — Mexico City. The surveyor, Alonso Garcia Bravo, laid out the great streets, the palace of Cortes and the cathedral which form the heart of Mexico City today. Aztec buildings were flattened; today, only their foundations are sometimes found during modern rebuilding. Great houses were built for the Spaniards and their allies, including Marina.

Then Cortes had to find a way of making all of Mexico obedient. There were still less than 2,000 Spaniards in the whole country, though more came as news of the conquest reached the Caribbean and Europe. The Spaniards were lucky that disease and slaughter made it very hard for other hostile cities to offer much resistance. Many of them were attacked by Spaniards or by Indians on Cortes's side. There was no chance of revival for the fallen masters of Mexico.

Last, but certainly not least, Cortes had to keep order amongst his own unruly soldiers. The men were furious. So little gold had been found when the city fell that each man received only fifty *pesos* (the price of a crossbow) as reward for the whole campaign. First they turned on the helpless Cuauthemoc, scorching his feet in a fire to make him reveal where his treasure was hidden. He said nothing, probably because no more treasure existed. Cortes did nothing to stop this torture and may even have ordered it. Next the soldiers began to hint that Cortes himself had taken all the gold. One wrote a little verse on the whitewashed wall of his house:

> My soul is very sad
> And will be till that day
> When Cortes gives us back
> The gold he's hid away.

Cortes was not amused, especially as he really had taken by far the best share of land, slaves and anything else that had been found.

The cathedral of Mexico City is built on the site of the great temple of the Aztecs. The building in the photograph dates from 1573, but the church was founded by Cortes.

'Encomiendas'

Something had to be done. Some conquistadors were already moving on to explore new lands in the hope of better fortune; Mexico would be left unguarded. It was dangerous to give such men nothing. They were private volunteers. If they received no reward they might rebel against Charles V himself, let alone Cortes.

Cortes used a system he had seen in the West Indies. He set up *encomiendas*. Briefly, this meant that Cortes gave some Spaniards the right to settle in a particular district, and live comfortably on the tribute which Indian towns and villages in 'his' district had to pay him. In return he was supposed to protect 'his' Indians from cheats and robbers and, above all, see that they became Christian. The Spaniards said *encomiendas* were right because they helped to spread Christianity. In

A picture map showing some of the mission churches in Mexico. Some routes, natural features and animals are shown. The document comes from the Archive of the Indies in Seville. Note the direction signs for East and West, at left and right respectively.

fact many *encomenderos* treated the Indians as if they were slaves, making them drag and build and carry. Many died, sometimes from deliberate Spanish cruelty but more probably through lack of care and through epidemic diseases. Cortes thought that the system was the only one which would keep both Spaniards and Indians reasonably quiet; though he never seems to have wondered if the Spaniards had any right to conquer Mexico in the first place, let alone do as they pleased with the inhabitants.

The cathedral at Cuernavaca, which dates from the time of Cortes. He also built a very large house here, but this has been almost completely altered since the sixteenth century.

Franciscan friars were responsible for most of the missionary work in Mexico. This is another Aztec drawing in Diego Duran's History.

Because the Aztecs wrote in pictures, Christian missionaries used picture-writing to help spread the Gospel. The pictures below include a bird (for the Holy Ghost) and the crucified Christ. This second kind of picture is unusual. In the early days the missionaries used plain crosses in case the Indians thought that Christians practised human sacrifice as the Aztecs did.

More illustrations from the early historian Bernadino de Sahagun. Indians are planting (left) and gathering (right) corn, their main food.

Cortes defeats Velasquez

While Cortes had been fighting Montezuma, his old enemy Diego Velasquez had not been idle. When Panfilo de Narvaez had been defeated Velasquez knew he could not overthrow Cortes by force. His best plan was to try and persuade Charles V that Cortes was really a rebel. He had many friends at court; so did Cortes. He sent messengers, letters and bribes; so did Cortes. What Velasquez could not do was present Charles V with an empire and its treasures. This was Cortes's trump card. Although many of the magnificent objects he sent to Charles had been captured by a French pirate (later hanged), enough had appeared to convince the emperor that Cortes had done well. His letters flattered the emperor and also made it seem that Cortes was not only successful, but honest, just and merciful too. We know that Cortes distorted the truth, as well as failing to mention that he had disobeyed Diego Velasquez (Charles's own governor in Cuba). He had several times been harsh, perhaps needlessly savage, to the Mexicans; had supervised one massacre at a place called Cholula, and may perhaps have murdered four Aztec princes and even Montezuma himself. We do not know for certain the rights and wrongs, though Cortes's enemies were not slow to accuse him of all these things, and later on of poisoning the wife he had married in Cuba and hardly seen for years.

Yet he had taken an empire, when it seemed that Diego Velasquez had done nothing but hinder him.

In 1522 news came that Charles had acquitted him of Velasquez's charges that he was a rebel and, better still, confirmed him as governor and chief justice of New Spain, as the country was now called. He had come almost to the height of his fame and power.

Cortes sends out new expeditions

Although Cortes devoted most of 1522 to bringing Mexico fully under control he did not forget that a whole New World was still to be won. He was still a conquistador himself, and even the conquest of an empire did not seem to be enough. He began to encourage new explorations, which served the twin purposes of keeping dangerous men busy and far from Mexico City, and increasing the chances of finding great new empires to give to Charles V.

Two of these expeditions were to be especially important. Pedro de Alvarado was sent south to conquer and settle Guatemala. That region was inhabited mainly by the Maya, who had once been a highly civilised people. Their temples, silent and deserted in dense jungle, or opened up for tourists, are still a dramatic and wonderful sight.

Cristobal de Olid, who had fought very bravely in Mexico, was sent to explore Honduras, also a region in which the Maya had been settled for over a thousand years.

It is interesting to see that Cortes was now in the same position as Diego Velasquez had been. Instead of leading an expedition in person he was sending out others. His captains might turn independent and shut him out, as he had freed himself from Velasquez. In 1524 news reached Mexico City that Cristobal de Olid had done just that. He had declared himself an independent conqueror and claimed that Cortes's orders had no force over him any more. Indeed the wheel had gone full circle, because the man who persuaded Olid to defy Cortes was none other than Diego Velasquez himself. He met the young captain while Olid was recruiting men in Cuba. This was Velasquez's last sting (he died soon after), but so far as Cortes was concerned, the damage had been done. It drove Cortes into making a very big mistake.

The Honduras expedition

When Cortes heard about Olid he decided to go himself to Honduras and put down the rebellion. This was a very strange decision. Olid was not dangerous to Cortes and there was far more to do in Mexico City. We cannot tell what went on in Cortes's mind. Perhaps he thought Olid would really become another Cortes – with himself as Velasquez. Perhaps he suspected that Olid was on the edge of finding a kingdom so wonderful and rich that Cortes would be forgotten. Perhaps Cortes himself was sick of organising people and sitting behind a desk. All his life he had been a rover and an adventurer. Whatever the reason, he made a mistake.

He assembled a force of soldiers. Bernal Diaz says he was so popular and persuasive that hardly anyone he asked could bear to say no. Complete with gold dinner service, jesters, trade goods and a herd of pigs to serve as self-propelled dinners, Hernan Cortes vanished for two years into the unexplored jungles of Yucatan and Honduras.

Cortes travelled over some of the most difficult country in the world. The Indians he met drew maps and gave directions without having the faintest idea of their accuracy. If they

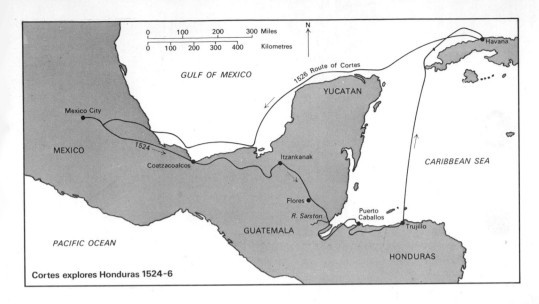

Cortes explores Honduras 1524-6

Cortes's route to Honduras was described in the 1540s by Gonzalo de Oviedo in his *Natural and General History of the Indies*, but we cannot be sure that it is accurate. Twenty years after Cortes's journey the country was still virtually unexplored.

below: Using canoes to ferry horses across a river, from Oviedo's history.

travelled it was by river, but Cortes went overland. He bridged over fifty rivers and struggled through hideous swamps. Diseases brought down even more men than usual.

Eventually a handful of starved, exhausted men staggered out of the jungle to the small settlement at the mouth of the Sarston. They found their sufferings had been unnecessary. Cortes's officer Francisco de las Casas had arrived by sea and managed to overpower and hang Olid. During the march Cortes himself had been wounded once more in the head and had suffered as much as any man. Yet even now he explored still more of Honduras, floating on a raft down-river while his crossbow men warded off hostile Indians.

Cortes returns to Mexico

When Cortes returned to the Spanish settlement in Honduras he learned that the Spaniards in Mexico City were fighting bitterly among themselves. He should not have left Mexico, for no one else had powers of leadership enough to keep the quarrelsome conquistadors in order, especially as some of them were vicious cut-throats. He returned by sea in May 1526.

He was able to put things to rights after a short struggle. He either hanged his enemies or persuaded them to obey him again. Still, damage had been done. While he had been away from the centre of power his enemies had been able to send back to Charles V in Europe all kinds of stories about him. Cortes himself simply said 'Long journeys, long lies,' but the mud stuck. He decided that his best plan would be to return to Europe himself; to see Charles face to face, as he had seen Montezuma, and claim again what he had won by force.

8 Cortes meets the emperor

In 1528 Cortes arrived at the Imperial Court. Charles V travelled all over his many kingdoms and at this time he was in Toledo. Cortes had left Spain almost penniless and completely unknown. He returned as a conquering hero. He had discovered an unknown world and given it to the emperor.

Charles was immensely grateful. He welcomed Cortes and his followers. Like many Europeans he was fascinated by stories and objects from the Americas. Cortes had brought many things the Aztecs had made as well as strange animals like these shown here.

Cortes received his reward. He was given the title of Marques del Valle, with vast lands in the Mexican province of Oaxaca. He had 30,000 Indian families living there. Indeed the area was so huge that later, when the government realised just how big it was, some was taken away, though much was still left. Most of all, he was given the right to hand his lands and titles on to his children and to their children for ever. This was very rare. No one else in Mexico was given that right except a few of Montezuma's closest relatives, each a great Aztec prince or princess.

Next Cortes put his family affairs to rights. His first wife Catalina Xuarez had died in Mexico. We know very little of this marriage. Some said it was unhappy, and even that Cortes poisoned her. Others told how he had lived a gay life with her in Cuba and 'howled like a dog' when he found her dead. His second marriage was arranged to suit his new rank. His bride was Dona Juana Zuniga. She was beautiful and, more important, her family had been nobles for generations. Cortes was 'in' socially.

Cortes also brought Montezuma's surviving daughters to Spain and saw them married off to noble Spaniards. In fact many of the Aztec nobility intermarried with Spaniards during the sixteenth century and formed a new aristocracy in Mexico.

Cortes had at least five illegitimate children (including Marina's son). They could not inherit unless the pope would agree to declare them legitimate. His Holiness said he would be

Armadillo (above), and opossum. Two of the strange new animals Cortes brought back from the New World.

happy to do so. Cortes thanked him by sending an Indian juggler to Rome to put on a special show. This delighted the pope and many cardinals who turned up to watch.

To crown it all, when Cortes was ill the Emperor Charles actually came and visited *him* – a very rare mark of honour and affection.

Shortly after Charles left for his coronation as Holy Roman Emperor Cortes departed for Mexico, taking his new wife, presents and glory with him. He had reached the highest point of his life. He was about 44 years old.

Cortes had been brave, charming, cunning, ruthless and very lucky. Even as he sailed away one of his bravest captains, Gonzalo de Sandoval, lay dying – too weak to prevent the landlord of the inn where he stayed from stealing the gold bars he had won with blood in Mexico. Cortes was sorry when he heard, but it was still everyone for himself in those hard times. All over Spain and the New World there were men like Sandoval, matched by thousands of Aztecs who had died or been made slaves for resisting the invasion of their country.

The death of Sandoval.

9 Cortes loses his power

Charles V liked and admired Cortes but he was not prepared to allow him to become king of Mexico. A difficult problem for the kings of Spain was how to control a vast empire so many thousands of miles away. The conquistadors were quarrelsome and undisciplined. Charles wanted them kept in order, the Indians protected – and the gold and silver of Mexico brought back safely to pay his soldiers in Europe.

Therefore he began to edge out the conquistadors, step by step, and replace them with officials sent from Spain. These men had taken no part in the conquest. They were loyal to Charles and they owed their whole careers to him. They respected the swordsmen who had won Mexico, but they put their duty to the emperor first.

The right men were not easy to find. Charles made several bad mistakes, appointing people who were worse than those they were supposed to govern. In 1535 he made no mistake. Mexico was declared to be a kingdom, just like Charles's territories in Europe. Since Charles could not be in every place at once he appointed a viceroy to govern each kingdom for him. Viceroys themselves took their orders direct from Charles, but it took so long to communicate with him that each viceroy was his own master in many ways.

The first viceroy of New Spain was Don Antonio de Mendoza. This man outranked everyone in Mexico, even Cortes, by birth and by holding the rank of viceroy. He was determined to be master of Mexico and reduce even Cortes's power. He had to move carefully because Cortes was not only popular with Spaniards but also the only man the Indians seem to have trusted.

More expeditions

Cortes was intelligent enough to realise what was happening. He became frustrated and bored. He turned more to another old interest, exploration and discovery. For years he had paid for ships to be built and ordered his crews to explore the

Don Antonio de Mendoza (?1490—1552), Viceroy of New Spain, 1535—50. He gradually took over power in Mexico for Charles V and put New Spain firmly under the control of Madrid. He was so successful that he was sent to do the same sort of work as Viceroy of Peru in 1551.

Pacific coast. There were two great prizes which might be won. First, everyone hoped to find new lands of gold, rich empires which would seal a man's rank and fortune forever. Cortes knew that nothing would make him the hero of the hour once again more quickly than such a find. The second prize, equally valuable, was to discover a strait linking the Caribbean or the

Cortes's coat of arms as Marques del Valle. The double eagle refers to Charles V as Holy Roman Emperor. Other devices refer to the conquest of Mexico: three gold crowns for the defeated alliance of Tenochtitlan, Texcoco and Tacuba; a city on the water; seven heads in a padlocked chain for seven kings conquered.

Gulf of Mexico directly with the Pacific. We know that such a strait does not exist in nature, and this sea link between the two great oceans did not come until the opening of the Panama canal in 1914. Yet the Spaniards hunted unceasingly in the sixteenth century.

In 1535 Cortes himself sailed northwards up the coast to search the bay of California. The sea was cobalt blue, the coast mostly desert with but a few poor Indian inhabitants. There was no strait to the Atlantic. His supply ships were wrecked, he nearly starved and found nothing worth mentioning.

Even these efforts aroused Mendoza's suspicion and rivalry. He sent expeditions of his own north and into the Pacific and although, in 1535, Cortes sent ships out to the Moluccas, his efforts as an explorer petered out. His last major occupation had disappeared. The Spanish government was no longer willing to take the risk that a man who had achieved what Cortes had managed might be allowed to win yet further glory.

Return to Spain

Eventually Cortes grew sick of Mexico. His estates in Oaxaca, especially the sugar plantations, were very successful. He was not able to export sugar to Europe as he had hoped, but his lands and palaces in Mexico City and Cuernavaca were still fit for a prince. Wealth was not enough. He needed action, employment. In 1540 he returned again to Spain. Once more Charles welcomed him. The Council of the Indies, who ruled the empire he had helped to win, treated him with deep respect. Special messengers invited him to their meetings. Yet he was offered no real authority of any kind.

left: the last part of Cortes's will, dated 11 October 1547, with his signature as Marques del Valle. Below are the signatures of two witnesses.

This savage caricature of Cortes and his men, by Diego Rivera in the National Palace, Mexico City, tells us little about the conquistadors. It does reveal how a twentieth-century revolutionary artist felt about the Church and the ruling class which the conquest planted firmly in Mexico.

In 1541 he joined Charles's expedition against the Algiers pirates. The fleet was shipwrecked. Cortes lost much, including eight huge emeralds he had brought from Mexico. Worse than this was the blow to his pride when the emperor did not even consult him about what was to be done next. It was not spite that made Charles neglect Cortes. A more likely reason is that kings of Spain never let any subject start thinking that the king could not do without him. It was also twenty years since he had taken Mexico. A new generation had grown up around the emperor. Cortes was getting old.

Retirement and death

The rest of his story is soon told. He had led an exhausting life, often starved, sleepless and several times wounded. He had borne the responsibility of leading an army and taking an empire. He had come through the hideous jungles of Honduras. He had seen his power taken away from him. He seems to have become more serious. The religious streak which was always in in him is easier to see. He began to prepare for death.

His last job was to put his affairs in order before he died. This was not easy. He became very tired and began to write rather sad letters to the emperor asking for help before it was too late. 'My work has made me content because I have done my duty, but it has failed to give me rest in my old age. It is making me work till I die.' 'I am sixty and have only a single son to come after me. If God disposed of this one, what profit would I have from everything I have gained in my lifetime? For if daughters inherit, the memory (of their father) is lost.'

There spoke the true hidalgo. These men desperately wanted their titles of nobility so that they would be remembered by generations after them. This mattered as much to men like Cortes as sacks of money.

He did arrange matters, shortly before he died of a stomach illness at his house near Seville on 2 December, 1547. He was about 63 years old.

In his will he asked to be buried in Mexico. His one legitimate son, Martin, inherited his estates and title of Marques del Valle. All his other children were provided for by money and suitable marriages. He left money to found a hospital, convent and school to care for the bodies and souls of the people of Mexico.

His remains are still in Mexico City, at his hospital. A small brass plate marks the spot where he is buried. It is hard to find because many modern Mexicans think of him as an invader and destroyer of their country. There is a great statue in the main avenue of Mexico City but it is to Cuauhtemoc, last emperor of the Aztecs, not Hernan Cortes.

Hernan Cortes c. 1484–1547

Cortes rose by bravery, daring, foresight and intelligence from nothing to almost the highest power. He had overthrown one emperor and given his prize to another. He had achieved the ambitions of every hidalgo; riches, power, fame for himself and his descendants. He was wonderfully charming to men and women. His power of personality made him a great leader. Above all he had two kinds of courage; the kind which enables a man to hang on and fight no matter what odds are against him *and* the kind which will go all out for complete victory or total defeat.

Yet there was another side. He had betrayed Velasquez. He had many times persuaded a man of one thing and then done another. He was certainly involved in one massacre and maybe another. He cheated his men of their share of the profits of the conquest time and time again. He was religious, but he did not allow his feelings to stop him looking after number one, always.

Last (and some would say greatest of all) he helped to destroy one of the most beautiful cities and remarkable civilisations in the world, without any provocation and need. The Aztecs were savage in religion and aggressive in warfare yet very advanced in other ways. Modern Mexicans find it impossible to forgive Cortes for what he did.

It is doubtful if he was ever sorry. Spaniards of his time saw their religion and civilisation as far greater than any other. Yet he may have seen a poem the broken-hearted Aztecs wrote about their ruined country and wondered, when his own power was lost, if the words applied to him also:
'Have you grown weary of your servants?
Are you angry with your servants,
O Lord,
O Giver of Life?'

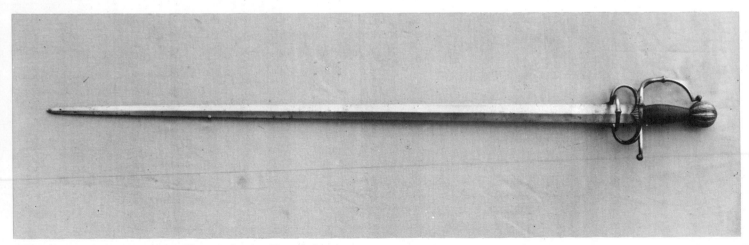

This sixteenth-century sword, now in the Royal Armoury, Madrid, is thought to have belonged to Cortes.

Index

Acknowledgments

Illustrations in this volume are reproduced by kind permission of the following:
back cover, pp.22 (right), 29 Trustees of the British Museum; pp.3, 27, 28, 39 (right), 45, 47 Jefe del Depto. de Relaciones Publicas del Instituto Nacional de Antropologia e Historia, Mexico; p.4 (top) Spanish Tourist Office; p.4 (bottom) Caroline Meynell; pp.7, 11 Ampliaciones y Reproducciones Mas, Barcelona; pp.14, 21, 37, 39 (top left) J. Allan Cash; pp.17, 39 (bottom left) Biblioteca Medicea Laurenziana, Florence, photo Dr. G. B. Pineider; p.18 Mexican National Tourist Council; p.19 (right) Cambridge University Library; pp.19 (left), 23 (right) Osterreichische National-bibliothek, Vienna; p.20 Stephen Harrison; p.22 (left) National-museet, Copenhagen; p.38 Archivo General de Indias, Seville; p.41 Huntington Library, San Marino, California; p.43 Zoological Society of London; p.46 Archivo of the Protocol, Seville; p.48 Foto-graphifia cedida y auturizida por el patrimonia nacional, Spain.

Drawings and cover illustration
by Graham Humphreys

front cover: Cortes at Otumba, as imagined by a modern artist. His immediate opponent is a 'Jaguar Knight' wielding a war-club (*macquauitl*) edged with obsidian blades.

back cover: A diagram of Tenochtitlan and its surroundings, printed in 1523 and supposedly based on a sketch by Cortes himself. The drawing is badly out of scale, but it does give a vivid impression of the position of the most important features of the city as they appeared to the Spaniards.

**Key to the Diagram
on the Back Cover:**

1 Southern causeway to Ixtapalapa, the road by which the Spaniards first came to the city

2 Western causeway to Tacuba

3 Northern causeway to Tepeyacac

4 Port for canoes plying to Texcoco

5 Dykes for protection against floods

6 Aqueduct carrying main water supply from the springs of Chapultepec

7 Main square of Tenochtitlan

8 Main square of Tlatelolco, the northern half of the city

9 Sacred enclosure, with temples, skull racks and an idol (shown without a head)

10 Montezuma's palace

11 Montezuma's garden

12 Montezuma's menagerie

13 Montezuma's pleasure-gardens outside the city

The Cambridge History Library

The Cambridge Introduction to History
Written by Trevor Cairns

The Cambridge Topic Books
General Editor Trevor Cairns

The Cambridge History Library will be expanded in the future to include additional volumes. Lerner Publications Company is pleased to participate in making this excellent series of books available to a wide audience of readers.

Lerner Publications Company
241 First Avenue North, Minneapolis, Minnesota 55401

#9462